No More Victims!
An Underdog Who Came Out on Top Challenges You to Put a Stop to Bullying in Your School

Frank Peretti

W PUBLISHING GROUP™

www.wpublishinggroup.com

A Division of Thomas Nelson, Inc.
www.ThomasNelson.com

No More Victims!

Produced with the assistance of The Livingstone Corpora-
tion. Project staff includes Joan Guest, Kathy and Tom
Ristow, Ashley Taylor, and Dana Veerman.

ISBN 084994337X

contents

1
Gym Class

A separate room had been prepared for the boys. It was cold and impersonal. The echoing, concrete walls had been painted beige, then marred and chipped over the years, and then painted again. The walls were bare except for posted rules, warnings, and advisories, and the only windows were high against the ceiling, caged behind iron grillwork thickly wrapped in paint, rust, and more paint. The air was dank, tainted with the odors of steam, sweat, and skin. Years of rust and sediment from the dripping showerheads and armies of bare, wet feet had marbled the floor with streaks and patches of reddish brown.

The authorities, clad in uniforms and carrying clipboards and whistles, marched the boys in, at least forty of them, all roughly the same age but many different sizes, strengths, and levels of maturity. The dates of their births, the locations of their homes, and the simple luck of the draw had brought them here, and much like cattle earmarked for shipment, they had no voice in the matter. The paperwork was in. This room would be a part of their lives for the next four years.

He had never been in this place, or anywhere like this place, before. He had never imagined such a place could even exist. In here, kindness meant weakness, human warmth was a complication, and encouragement was unmanly. In here, harshness was the guiding virtue—harshness, cruelty, and the blunt, relentless confirmation of every doubt he'd ever carried about himself.

Mr. M, a fearsome authority figure with a permanent scowl and a voice that yelled—only yelled—ordered them to strip down. His assistants, clones of his cruelty, repeated the order, striding up and down the narrow aisles between the lockers.

The boy hesitated, looking furtively about. He'd never been naked in front of strangers before, but even worse, he'd never been naked in front of enemies. It had taken only one hour in gym class for the others to select him, to label him, and to put him in his place. He was now officially the smallest one, the scared one, the weakling, the one without friends. That made him fair game when it came time for showers.

Now he would be naked in front of them. Naked. His stomach wrung; his hands trembled. *Please, God, get me out of here. Please don't let them do this to me.*

But every authority figure in his life had said he had to be here. He had to go to school, do his chores, finish his homework, keep his shoes tied, go to bed and get up at certain hours, eat his vegetables, and be here. End of discussion.

He removed his clothes.

Mr. M continued his yelling. "Come on, move it, move it, move it!"

The herd—pink, black, brown, and bronze—moved in one direction, and all he could do was move with it, a frail, naked body among the forty, longing for a towel, anything to cover himself. Every other body was bigger and stronger, and every other body had hair where the boy had none. He knew they would notice.

The showers were a long, high-ceilinged echo chamber, murky with steam, rattling with lewd, raucous joking and laughter. He didn't want to hear it.

After a big kid finished his shower, the boy carefully took his place under the showerhead, afraid of slipping and even more afraid of grazing against anyone. He let the water spray over him. He hurriedly lathered his body with some soap.

To his left, the talk started about him. Then some laughing. The talk spread, the call went out, "Hey, get a load of this!" An audience gathered, a semicircle of naked, dripping bodies. The talk about him shifted to jeering at him. He tried to act as if he didn't hear them, but he could feel his face flushing. *Get through, get through, get out of here!*

He rinsed as well as he could, never turning away from the wall, then headed for the towel-off area, not meeting their eyes, trying to ignore their comments about his face, his body, his groin. But the arrows were landing with painful accuracy: "Ugly." "Wimp." "Gross." "Little girl."

He grabbed a towel off the cart and draped it around himself before he even started drying with it. Even that action brought lewd comments and another lesson: Once it begins, no action, no words, no change in behavior will turn it back. Once you're the target, anything you do will bring another arrow.

And so the arrows flew: two, then three, then more. Obscenities, insults, put-downs.

Along with his hurt, he felt a pitiful, helpless anger.

He wanted to lash out, to tell them to stop, to defend himself, but he was too aware of his body, just as they were. He could never match the strength of any one of them, much less the whole gang, and they were waiting for him, even wanting him, to try.

Snap! Stinging pain shot up from his legs like a jolt from an electric cattle prod.

"Oh," hollered a jock, "good one!"

Snap! He heard the sound again as a towel whipped past his backside, missing by a millimeter. A big lug with a hideous grin pulled his towel back for another try, then he jerked it toward the boy's body again, snapping it back hard, turning the moist end of the towel into a whip. The edge of the towel struck between the boy's legs.

He cried out in pain while they laughed. He raised a knee to protect himself but lost his footing on the wet tile and tumbled to the floor, his hands skidding on the slimy, soapy residue. He struggled to his feet. A wet foot thumped into his back, and he careened toward a locker-room bench loaded with laughing bodies.

"Get off me, you fag!" Rough hands pushed him and he crunched into another body. "Get away, twerp!" They were angry with him. He was the Ping-Pong ball being batted about, and they were angry with him!

"Hey, squirt, you lookin' for trouble?"

"I think this kid wants a fight!"

He fled to the only square foot of floor that might be his own, the space in front of his locker. His body was throbbing. And his soul . . . He was choking back tears, hurrying, fumbling to get his clothes from his locker, resolving to remain silent, desperately hoping no one would see him crying, but deep inside his soul wailed in anguish, and there were no words or thoughts to heal it. Parental advice came to his mind, but it carried as much weight as a cookie fortune: "Just ignore them." Ignoring was only acting. It didn't stop the arrows from cutting through his heart. He even believed the taunts and stinging words. *Am I that ugly? Am I that weak and worthless?*

"Hey, nude boy! Hey, nature boy!" Now the teacher's assistant, just a few grades ahead of him, was getting in a few jabs. "Get the lead out. The bell's gonna ring in five minutes."

He got the lead out. Still wet, he threw on his clothes, missing one buttonhole in his shirt so that the shirt hung cockeyed, but he didn't care. He grabbed his books. Then a hand slammed him against the locker, and his head bounced off the steel door. His books fell to the floor, the pages crinkling, his assignments spilling everywhere. He'd only begun the thought of picking them up when one of the jocks grabbed him around the neck, lifted him off the floor so his feet dangled, then dropped him on his books. He crumpled to the floor, gasping.

A whistle shrieked. It was Mr. M, angry as always. "Line up, line up!"

The assistant yanked the boy to his feet. "C'mon, get in line!"

He gathered up his books, some of the pages wet, wrinkled, and grimy. One minute to go. He'd never felt such longing to be somewhere else. Somewhere in his memory—right now, a dim memory—was a kinder world than this, a place where he could find some measure of his lost dignity, the last tatters of his self-respect.

The bell rang. Mr. M swung the door open. The lines

started moving, a few boys at the front of the line dart-
ing off as though they were in a race for their lives.

"No running. WALK!" Mr. M growled.

The stream of bodies poured into the narrow hall, and
in a moment he was hurrying away from that place, taking several last looks over his shoulder, checking for dan-
ger, thankful he could still turn his neck.

In the main hall, he passed the trophy case, where the
glories of his high school were on display. Here were the
school colors, pictures of the school mascot, the trophies,
the ribbons, the news clippings, the victories: everything
a kid should be proud of. His eyes flooded with tears.
When he first came to this school, he looked in that trophy case, and, yes, he was proud. He was filled with an
exhilarating joy and a sense of belonging. School spirit,
that's what it was. He couldn't wait to buy a pennant to
hang on the wall of his room.

But now, all he could do was shed tears and wonder,
*How could a school like this, my school, be like that? Does
anyone care? Does anyone even know?*

In his next class, he sat at his desk, his clothes still
damp, his body still aching, unable to keep his mind on
the teacher's lecture or his eyes on the text. The mocking faces and the derisive comments kept replaying in
his mind, overpowering anything and everything else.

In the loneliness of his hurt and anger, little thoughts
were firing off in his mind like forbidden firecrackers: *Oh,
right, Mr. Assistant, sir, Mr. Big Tough Guy, Mr. M in
miniature. You wouldn't be so tough if Mr. M weren't
around. And as for you, Superjock and Dumb Thug and
Towel Turkey, if I were bigger, if I were stronger, if I could
. . . if I could . . . oh, man, if only I could . . .*

But he wasn't supposed to think such things, so he tried not to. He was supposed to be a good kid.

He said nothing, and he did nothing, and when the day for gym class came around again, he went back. After all, the authorities in his life had made clear certain axioms: He had to be there. There was no choice.

2
How It All Began

I was born in a country hospital in the middle of a huge blizzard. The hospital staff thought I'd take my time coming into the world, so no one paid much attention to my mom while she was in labor. By the time the doctor arrived, the labor had become complicated.

After my birth it became clear that there was something wrong. I had a lump on my neck and my head would not move naturally. I did not eat properly either and was not gaining weight. After I was taken home, the lump began to grow. The local medical people all said it was nothing to worry about, but my parents were not convinced.

In God's providence—so mysterious yet so painful at the time—Dad's ministry at the little country church that he pastored came to an end, and it was time to move on. Dad's folks, my grandparents, lived in Seattle, so we traveled there to live with them while Mom and Dad figured out the next direction for their life and family. Concerned that the lump on my throat was growing, Mom took me to a Seattle doctor to get a second opinion. This physician took one look at my neck and declared emphatically, "We need to get him to the hospital right away!"

My parents took me to Children's Orthopedic

Hospital in Seattle, where the doctors quickly diagnosed my condition. *Cystic hygroma* is a birth defect. The lymph system is like the circulatory system only it carries fluid through the body instead of blood. In cystic hygroma the lymph system around the head and neck doesn't form correctly, so fluids get backed up and clogged and then infection grows. In most cases this creates a bulge or cyst that keeps growing. In my case, this malformation had allowed fluid to build up around my windpipe. I could barely breath, and it had also affected my eating. Cystic hygroma can also cause shaking, bleeding, and infection, and I was showing signs of developing all of these by the time the doctor recognized what was happening. It was time to operate.

I was barely two months old when the doctors cut my neck open, trying to clean out a swollen mass that threatened to kill me. They succeeded and then kept me in the hospital for ten days to watch for possible complications. It must have been a long haul for a newborn. Mom recalls that when they finally placed me back in her arms to go home, I was a tiny "bag of bones," with a long scar and black sutures that made it appear as if my head had been nearly severed and then sewn back on.

"We've done all that we can," the doctors told my parents. "Take him home and love him, and that will be the best medicine for him." Although the doctors informed Mom and Dad that a recurrence was possible and that cystic growth into surrounding tissues was unpredictable, they didn't expect any complications.

Mom and Dad got back to building their life, and we did all right. Thanks to the love of my folks and my older brother, Terry, I fattened up again just fine.

But then came complications that the doctors didn't expect. As they'd said, cystic growth can be unpredictable, and the unpredictable happened. My tongue began to swell, and before long, it was hanging out of my mouth, oozing a fluid that turned to black scab when it dried. I drooled constantly, leaving bloody, blackish residue around my mouth and chin, down the front of my clothes, and on my pillow. I was having trouble eating. Imagine trying to swallow or chew without the help of your tongue!

I became a frequent and familiar patient at Children's Orthopedic Hospital. The doctors feared cancer, but one elderly surgeon had seen my symptoms previously in another patient, a little girl, whose precious face had been hideously distorted due to her condition. The doctor guessed that the swelling in my tongue was the result of my earlier operation, during which the cyst had been removed. Some lymph glands had also been removed, so now my body was oozing infection into my tongue.

It was going to be a tough problem to fix. With the tongue so enlarged, there was no way to shrink it down again except to carve it down. In the first of many operations on my tongue and mouth, the doctors literally cut a wedge of flesh from my tongue in an effort to keep it in my mouth.

With my tongue carved down to a stump, however, it couldn't do the usual tasks a tongue is supposed to do. I could barely move it. Eating was difficult, speaking even more so. The surgeons operated again and again, removing flesh below my tongue to free it up, then performing plastic surgery on my face around my jaw and chin. By the time I was four years old, I had endured seven rounds of surgery. I vaguely remember some of the later operations; I can still recall how unpleasant it felt, being tied to a hospital bed, being fed through tubes shoved down my nose, and having wooden sleeves holding my arms straight so I couldn't touch my face. I missed my family, I wanted to go home, and I wanted to sleep in real pajamas, not those goofy hospital gowns that are wide open in the back.

When at last the doctors allowed me to go home, the journey wasn't over. My tongue was still big and unwieldy, protruding from my mouth, and by now I was learning to talk that way. My speech was slurred, like Sylvester the Cat, and my tongue was still oozing fluid that caked on my lips and chin like dark chocolate, and sometimes sprayed on others if I pronounced a really strong *s*. I drew stares wherever we went. Mom, Dad, and my brother, Terry, were protective, but they couldn't possibly shield me from the natural disgust most people expressed, knowingly or not, once they noticed the raw flesh and brown gunk in my mouth.

"Ooh, what's wrong with him?" the children, and too often the adults, would say. "Ooh, yuck!"

When I consider my condition at the beginning, I can see how fortunate I was. For a while, the doctors were concerned that my face would be misshapen or that my teeth would come in crooked because of the constant pressing of my tongue, but amazingly, my face maintained its normal structure, and my teeth came in straight. It could have been a lot worse. In researching cystic hygroma, I've found that other kids with the defect have had to bear much greater burdens.

My burden was limited to my ugly tongue and one

side effect: my small stature. Apparently, my body had been so preoccupied with fighting off infection that it had to postpone growing. The doctors assured my folks that I'd catch up eventually. We would just have to be patient.

Mom and Dad loved my brother and me, and we played together and got into fights. Our younger brother, Paul, came along, and Terry and I got jealous because Paul got to have Ivory soap in his bath and we didn't.

I was small and I talked funny, but that didn't matter at home. Mom and Dad always loved me and let me know that I was special, that I would grow up to be big and strong someday, and that the problem with my tongue would soon go away. I believed them, and we did all right.

Then I had to go to school.

3
Monsters on the Brain

"**C**ome on, honey. It's time to go to school," I heard Mom's voice calling. "You are going to have so much fun. You'll get to color and play games and listen to stories. You'll love it!"

Mom checked my sweater to make sure I was dressed just right for my first day of kindergarten. My tongue still protruded from my mouth, and I had difficulty pronouncing many words, but I had developed my own way of saying words when my tongue refused to cooperate. For the most part, I could communicate fairly well.

Going to kindergarten was almost like being at home. The teacher was kind and loving, and she never said a word about my disfigurement. At first, most of the children were kind, too, or maybe they were just as awed by the school experience as I was, so I didn't receive many snide remarks. As the year went on, however, the teasing began.

Children can say the funniest things. They also can say some of the cruelest things imaginable. Even at that young age, the kids seemed compelled to remind me about the scab-covered tongue hanging from my mouth.

By the end of my kindergarten year, I'd had quite enough of school and didn't want to return.

When Mom dropped me off at school to begin first grade, I decided not to stay. By now, I was extremely self-conscious about my size and deformity, so as soon as I saw our car disappear around the corner, I ran away from school and headed back home. I was like a human boomerang, returning to the person who sent me out. Sometimes I got home before Mom parked the car in our garage!

"I don't wanna go to school!" I railed.

"Frank, honey, you have to go to school," Mom insisted.

"No, I'm not going!"

"Yes, you must."

I loved my mother dearly, and she loved me, even as she planted deeply in my mind the axioms of authority that would follow me for years: "You have to be there. You have no choice."

She herded me into the car and drove me back to school.

One morning, after I ran away from school again and Mom took me back, my teacher told her, "You just leave him to me. I'll handle him."

Mom peeked through the window of the door to the classroom while the teacher took me back inside and kindly but firmly sat me down at my desk. I burst out in tears and wailed wildly. The teacher remained nonplussed. She gave me some special assignments and told me, "Now, Frank, stop your crying. You're in school now. It's time to do your work like a big boy." The teacher arranged my work on the desk for me and gave me enough to keep me busy for a while. She checked on me regularly, and before long, I became interested in the work and forgot about the incessant teasing of the other children.

Until recess, when it started all over again.

This scenario was repeated throughout my elementary school years. On one occasion, Mom and Dad complained to the school principal about the teasing. The principal listened attentively and apparently passed the word on to some teachers, but no amount of adult supervision could prevent the arrows from piercing my heart on the playground, in physical education class, or in the school bathrooms, away from the watchful eyes of the teachers.

The only safe havens were home and church. The kids at church had known me most of my life and understood that something was wrong. They were good friends. They had heard some of the adults praying for my healing, and some of them had even prayed for me themselves.

One Sunday morning, when I was about seven years of age, I was sitting in church, trying to keep from squirming around as Dad led the song service. My tongue was throbbing. Intense pain began to flare around my throat. Before long, I felt as if a lump of meat was stuck in my throat and I could barely breathe.

We weren't supposed to talk in church. We weren't supposed to fidget or make noise. So, since I had to scream and cry, I did it while running out of the sanctuary.

Mom came running after me. "Frank! What's wrong?"

I clutched at my throat, choking, tears streaming from my eyes. The more I cried, the worse the pain got. Mom took one look at my neck and saw the swelling around my throat.

19

Mumps!* A serious enough affliction for any child, but far worse for a child with cystic hygroma! Mom raced to a phone and called our doctor, who prescribed medication to reduce the fever and swelling.

The medication did the trick and I was able to breathe more easily, but getting any food past my doubly swollen tongue and badly constricted throat was another matter. Mom and Dad had to feed me through a straw for several weeks. My bout with the mumps served to notify them that I was probably going to need more surgery on my tongue and mouth.

And so it went. Life was painful at times because of sickness, the world was cruel at times because of taunts and teasing, and the laundry could get gruesome whenever my tongue decided to have another "eruption."

But I have to brag about my mom and dad. Along with the Lord, they were the solid rock under my feet and never neglected any chance to encourage my creativity. I became interested in drawing and cartooning, so they supplied me with paper, pencils, and art books. I wanted to build a twenty-foot model of the Titanic in the backyard, so Dad let me use his tools and scrap lumber—provided I put everything away when I was done. My brothers and I set out to build some airplanes in the garage, so Dad moved the cars out and let us have at it. We were going to build a foot-powered paddleboat as well, but only got as far as stacking some big old oil

---

* Mumps was a common childhood illness when I was a kid, but now it is usually prevented by a vaccination. The primary symptom is huge swollen glands in the neck.

drums for flotation on the back patio for several months. I came up with an idea for a gas-powered, one-man blimp (like the Goodyear one that flies over football games), but that never got started.

Most of our big projects never floated or flew. Usually, we'd go nuts on one project for a few weeks, then we'd tear it all apart so we could use the lumber and nails to fulfill the next big vision. Mom and Dad just watched to make sure we didn't hurt ourselves, made sure we put things away and got our homework done, and went with the flow. Dad gave us advice, let us use his tools, and granted us room in the garage, on the patio, or in the basement, for as long as it took. Never once did he tell us it wasn't worth it or that we'd never succeed or that our ideas were dumb.

We had a great lab in the basement, full of jars, bottles (mostly empty canning jars and ketchup bottles with dyed water inside), and cool mad-scientist gadgetry (a dead television, the insides from an old tube radio, the chopper from a broken cider press). We'd crayoned a brick pattern on the concrete walls and hung some of Mom's nylon stockings from the ceiling to simulate stalactites. Zenarthex, our Frankenstein-like model, had his own slab (a door lying on orange crates) and a super electrical heart zapper (an empty can of talcum powder fastened to a length of gooseneck conduit with duct tape). We thought it might have been cool to get a red light bulb for the ceiling or maybe one of those Christmas tree floodlights with a rotating, colored disk to add some mood to the place, but this was a cheap operation. We'd built all this stuff in hopes of making our own low-budget monster movie.

Monsters were my friends. My associates. My obsession. By now, I was just on the brink of thirteen. It was the 1960s. John F. Kennedy had been assassinated, the Beatles had just invaded, skirts were short, and pants were tight. My younger brother, Paul, and I had expanded our territories to the point of war in our old room, so now he had his own room, and I had mine.

But I was not alone in my room. Frankenstein was there, both as a wall poster and as a plastic model on my desk. I had other plastic models, as well, each meticulously assembled and painted: Dracula, gesturing hypnotically; the Creature from the Black Lagoon, poised to scratch someone's face off; the Mummy, all wrapped up and rotten; the Phantom of the Opera, singing an aria with his mask in his hand; the Hunchback of Notre Dame, bleeding from a whipping; the Witch, stirring up a potion in her pot. I had posters of monsters, monster masks, monster magazines, and monster comic books. I wrote stories and drew comics about monsters and mad scientists; I told the neighbor kids stories about dead bodies and spooks, and I made audio dramas on my folks' old reel-to-reel tape recorder about devious, monster-stitching, body-snatching scientists with silly foreign accents.

The monsters were ugly, misunderstood, abused—creatures who escaped from their cages, traps, and laboratories, scared everyone, broke things, and got back at the unfeeling people who abused them. They may have been victims, but they turned around and made victims of others. The Frankenstein monster was tormented relentlessly by Igor, Dr. Frankenstein's humpbacked assistant, but the monster got even. The Creature from the

Black Lagoon was captured and imprisoned in a huge aquarium, but he finally clawed his way out of there and got some respect. Both the Phantom of the Opera and the Hunchback of Notre Dame were scarred, ugly, and misunderstood, but at least for one poignant, wishful, intense moment, they had the appreciation of the girl.

No wonder I kept those guys around. Somewhere in my head, planted there repeatedly over the years, was the notion that I was one of them—ugly, rejected, picked on, and somehow less worthy of membership in the world of normal kids. I was entering adolescence, that weird age when the size, shape, and appearance of your body mean everything, and everyone seemed to be growing except me. On the right side of my neck, a visible scar and a depression could be seen where once there had been a tumor. Because of the problem with my tongue, I spoke with an obvious lisp and often mangled words when my mind darted faster than my mouth could follow. I wore glasses and one of two favorite vests every day, and let's face it, if I wasn't a bona fide nerd, I sure came close. Girls? Once I lamented to my mom, "I'm so ugly, nobody would ever want to marry me!"

And the torment from my classmates continued. All of them bigger and proud of it, they would take special pleasure in making my life miserable. I was pushed, shoved, thrown, hit, insulted, badgered, manhandled, teased, and harassed, and just as any monster must get tired of everyone screaming at the first sight of him, I was tired of kids asking, "Ooh, what's wrong with your tongue?" before they'd even ask me my name. Increasingly, through the eyes of others, I saw myself as a monster.

4
Why It Must Stop

Maybe you can relate to what I've been describing. Ever been there yourself? Maybe you're there right now, in a situation in which someone is constantly stabbing you with words, kicking you with cruel acts, hurting you, and taking away your dignity. You wish you could do something about it, get out of that situation, but all around you are those invisible walls, those axioms of authority that hold you in: "You have to be there. You have no choice. You have to go. You have to be in that situation. We can't change anything." You have to go to that school, sit in that classroom, eat in that lunchroom, or endure the taunts of that particular group.

Maybe you're the one who lies awake at night dreading every morning because of the people waiting for you at school. They have a name for you. It's not your real name; it's the one they gave you, something that labels you as inferior, ugly, or stupid. And there are others whom you don't even know, who don't know you, who call you by that name because it's fun for them. They have never bothered to ask you what your real name is. It's their mission to take away your dignity. They spit on you, trip you, knock the books out of your arms, and stomp on your ankles from behind. It doesn't matter what you wear, they laugh at it. If you own something new, they steal it, spill on it, tear it, and destroy it.

There is no particular reason for the torment. Any reason that can possibly be found or contrived will do. They pick on you because you're smaller, because you have a rare blood type, because you pick apples on your way home, you sing a particular song, you wear a particular sweater, you can't throw or catch a ball, you can't run fast, you don't have the right clothes, or simply because you're not like them.

In physical education class, your oppressors have the perfect opportunity to harass you because they're in close proximity, and all the activity is physical. It's a convenient time to take physical advantage of you because you're small or weak or maybe not so great an athlete or not yet physically developed. So they push you and shove you, throw you, kick you, trip you, and make fun of you.

Of course, there's nothing you like better than taking a shower or changing clothes with that bunch, being naked before your enemies, laid bare for them to spot your most intimate physical secrets so they can laugh at you, spread the word about you, torment you.

Those to whom you look for love, shelter, and protection tell you to ignore your tormentors, to stay away from them. Ignore them? Let's be honest: Ignoring is acting, and nothing more—acting as though the words or actions of your oppressors don't hurt. You hear the words, you feel the insults, and you bear the blows. You can act deaf and impervious to pain, but the stabs and the arrows pierce you anyway.

"Just stay away from them." Don't you wish that you

had a choice? Can you choose which lunchroom to sit in, which squad to line up in, which desk to sit at, which bus to ride home, or which direction to walk home?

If you say anything about the bullying you endure, you're a snitch or a wimp, and you only compound the problem. At least, that seems to be the universal, unwritten code of conduct.

If you had a choice, you wouldn't be there, but you don't have a choice. You are hemmed in by the rules and requirements of the adult world, the expectations placed upon you from birth. Of course, you obey, of course, you do what you're told, of course, you submit to authority and authority's axioms, and, yes, in many cases, that is as it should be.

By their indifference to abuse, bullying, and harassment, parents and teachers send subtle messages often written between the lines: You must also endure whatever comes with the package. It happens. Life is tough. Kids will be kids. We all went through it. It's part of growing up. It's a rite of passage. Get over it. It'll make you stronger. Suck it up, kid.

But wounds can fester. They can become infected, and then they can infect others. And they can change you because you haven't merely cut your finger or bruised your knee. You've been wounded in your spirit, and that wound pierces deeply, painfully, sometimes even permanently. When tough times or injuries come, we must be able to draw upon a reservoir of hope, faith, and self-confidence stored up inside us through the love and encouragement of friends and family. If enemies have drained that reservoir, the tough times will be even tougher.

At the time of this writing, I'm close to fifty years of age, but I still remember the names and can see the faces of those individuals who made my life a living nightmare, day after day after day, during my childhood. I remember their words, their taunts, their blows, their spittle, and their humiliations. As I review my life, I think of all the decisions I shied from, all the risks I dared not take, all the questions I never asked, all the relationships I didn't pursue, simply because I didn't want to be hurt again.

Moreover, I am haunted by the tragedy of Littleton, Colorado. We've all heard the many theories about why two students strode into Columbine High School and massacred their schoolmates and a teacher. I'm sure the theories about violence on television and movies, violent video and computer games, the availability of guns, and the unavailability of parents all have their legitimate place in the discussion. I don't pretend to know with certainty what was happening in the hearts and minds of those young killers, and yet . . .

I remember the thoughts I had, sitting alone in the school library after one bully picked me up by my neck or sitting alone on the street curb, eyes watering, after another kid sprayed deodorant in my face. I remember what I wished I could do if only I had the strength, the skill in martial arts, or the advantage that a baseball bat might give me over the bullies who bludgeoned and batted me around verbally and physically.

My monsters were a way to get back—in my imagination at least—at those who tormented me. But nowadays kids devise all sorts of monsters to identify with, and this new breed of monster will do almost anything for the power to change his situation and get even. Instead of getting into imaginary monsters, a modern-day victim of abuse can gravitate to violent video games, in which he can vent his pain and anger by blasting his enemies into atoms.

He or she can watch movies—so many movies!—in which the hero solves his situation by shooting everybody and blowing everything up. He might identify with a historical monster: Adolf Hitler, a tyrant who had total life-or-death control over millions, who could scare and terrorize people, and who could solve all his problems with violence. He can fill his mind with Nazi mythology, wear a black shirt with a swastika, speak German in the halls and on his Web pages, and talk about whom he hates and whom he'd like to kill. All this the killers in Columbine did. And then they killed their tormentors and many innocent people.

Why is it so important that we address the problem of bullying in our society? Because one in four bullies will end up in prison or the correctional system.[1] Because those who have been wounded often become those who wound others. Because we could be allowing the creation of more monsters—the kind you never see, never expect, until they snap and take desperate, violent measures. And all of us, those who have been wounded as well as those who wound others, need healing, forgiveness, and a new attitude toward our fellow human beings.

It's time for change.

So what can we do? We call it by many names: Abuse. Teasing. Taunting. Harassment. Bullying. Tormenting. Until now, we've been strangely quiet about it. "It happens," we say. "We all go through it. All the kids do it.

It's part of life. It's no big deal. It happened when we were kids."

Is it wrong? If the answer is yes, that immediately raises another question: Why do we allow it? Why do parents, teachers, teacher's assistants, fellow students, friends at school and church, coworkers, extended family members, and others see it happening, hear it happening, and know it's happening but fail to take it seriously? If devaluing human life—and thereby mocking God's creation—is wrong, why do so many people do so little to stop it? Worse yet, why do so many participate in it?

Surely my gym teacher was aware of what his students and his teacher's assistants were doing to that poor little kid in the shower. Surely the teachers and staff at Columbine—or any school for that matter—could hear the sounds of bodies hitting lockers, see the ketchup stains all over some students' clothing, and hear the laughter of the bullies and the cries of the victims. Surely the bus drivers know when a gang of losers descends on one helpless kid, knocking his books all over the street at the bus stop. Surely the teachers notice when a child comes into class with her shirt torn, her shoes missing, or her clothing soiled. Most certainly, the kids know what's happening; they're a part of it. They face the bullying, badgering, and other such treatment almost every day in school; they're immersed in it. Why don't they attempt to put a stop to it, to refrain from such behavior themselves, and to confront it in their friends?

What about the parents of children who are being bullied? Do they have no options? Do they have no voice? Must they sit by in silence when they know their child is near vomiting from stress before leaving for school each morning? Or are they even aware of the problem?

What about you? Are you being wounded senselessly, mercilessly, needlessly, by someone stronger than you, more powerful than you, someone who has leverage over you in some very real way?

Or are you the person who is doing the bullying, either openly or secretly?

It's time to talk about it. It's time for a change.

In the next chapter, I'll share a story with you that illustrates the absolute necessity for including Someone greater than ourselves in our world. If we really want to bring about change, this is where the change must begin.

5
The Imaginary Playground

It was the daddy of all playgrounds, stretching out acre upon acre and filled with laughing, playing children. Boys and girls were running, chasing, and screaming playfully. Jump ropes were spinning as kids chanted rhythmical rhymes; baseballs arched through the air, glove to hand, hand to glove, ball to glove, glove to ground. From the paved basketball and Four Squares area came the constant boing, boing, boing of balls bouncing from one child to another.

This was a happy place, usually. The kids played well together and followed the playground rules, most of the time. Sometimes a quarrel broke out, occasionally even an actual fight, but these skirmishes were quickly resolved. All in all, the playground was a wonderful, fun-filled environment for kids to enjoy.

The playground rules, clearly posted on a big wooden sign beside the entrance, helped to provide every recess with the desired peace, order, and domestic tranquillity. The rules were clear enough for any kid to understand:

NO HITTING.
NO PUSHING OR SHOVING.
NO FIGHTING.
SHARE THE EQUIPMENT.
TAKE TURNS.
NO SPITTING ON THE GIRLS.
NO CHASING THE BOYS.

The playground rules were sacred, omnipresent, and inscribed on every heart and mind; there was hardly a child there who hadn't had cause to appeal to those standards at one time or another.

For instance, when Jordan first arrived on the playground, he brought with him the idea that once the baseball was in his hand, he had total control over it. His would-be teammates tried to explain to him that unless he gave up possession of the baseball, there would be no baseball game. Reason alone would not change his mind. Appealing to the playground rules finally did.

Clyde always seemed to have extra saliva in his mouth and apparently felt compelled to put it somewhere else. Rachel was the nearest available depository, and he was happy to share with her out of his abundance, until she appealed to the playground rules, and he was required to swallow it.

The playground rules were the protector of the oppressed, the defender of the weak, the guarantor of social stability. Of course, we cannot overlook the importance of Mrs. Kravitz, the teacher on playground duty. Mrs. Kravitz represented the authority that put up those rules in the first place. Without her presence, the playground rules would have been nothing more than words painted on a board. She was sharp-eyed and elephant-eared, always ready to help in time of trouble but also ready to deal with troublemakers. She had a stern expression for that purpose, as well as a whistle, a clipboard, and a stack of pink slips that could mean a visit to the vice principal.

Some of the kids appreciated her presence on the playground, and, naturally, some of the kids preferred she not be there. The former felt secure; the latter felt imposed upon. But, like it or not, the playground was reasonably safe and orderly, because Mrs. Kravitz and the playground rules kept it that way.

Then one day something was different on the playground. It took a while for the kids to notice, but eventually they realized that Mrs. Kravitz was nowhere to be found. Some were glad, of course. "Good riddance!" they said. But some were concerned and asked the other teachers where Mrs. Kravitz had gone.

"Well," said the teachers, "we've decided that no one really has the right to tell you what to do. You kids are able to decide for yourselves the right thing to do. You have the capacity to solve all your own problems and make this a better playground. You don't need Mrs. Kravitz."

"But what about the playground rules?" they asked.

"You can decide for yourselves if the playground rules are right for you. It's really not our place to say that any one set of rules is better than another."

And so the kids were left to the whims of their own hearts. For a time, the playground rules still held sway in their minds. The rules worked well enough in the past; they continued to bring stability in the days that followed.

But one day Clyde stopped to consider the excess saliva in his mouth and whether or not he should swallow. "It's my mouth and my spit," he reasoned to himself. "I don't see what business anyone else has telling me how to get rid of it." Whereupon, he fired off a huge, undulating glob that hit Rachel right in the face.

Rachel was beside herself. She felt violated, betrayed, and insulted, not to mention wet and gross. "Clyde! You aren't supposed to do that!"

"Oh, yeah?" he responded. "Who says?"

She promptly took him over to the old sign displaying the playground rules.

"See here?" she said, pointing. "The rules say, 'No spitting on the girls.'"

"Well, I can choose to live by those rules or not."

"But you hurt me and you know it!"

"That depends on your definition of hurt."

Not long after this, the baseball game came to a screeching halt when Jordan caught a pop-up fly and abruptly walked off with the baseball.

"Hey," the others shouted, running after him, "that's our ball!"

"It's mine now," he replied.

"But you have to share!"

"Oh, yeah? Who says?"

They pointed to the rules. "It says, 'Share the equipment.'"

Jordan was unmoved. "You really believe that old sign? Come on, we don't need those rules. We can make our own rules now."

The other boys were stymied, except for those who weren't afraid of a little roughness. The rules didn't apply anymore, so . . . they ganged up on Jordan, knocked him to the ground, and got the baseball back.

Following Jordan's line of reasoning, Sally and Maria promptly took possession of a jump rope. The girls from whom they'd taken it tried to be open-minded and tolerant, but they still couldn't help feeling cheated somehow. "We think you should share," they said.

Sally rolled her eyes as Maria responded, "We think you should stop trying to impose your morality on us."

"But remember the rules?"

Sally and Maria laughed mockingly in the other girls' faces.

This new way of thinking caught on. The children had no need of authority or Mrs. Kravitz anymore. Each child was his or her own authority. As for the rules, although the standards on the old sign beside the playground never changed, the rules became increasingly irrelevant. The children finally tore down the sign.

When the first real fight broke out, Tracy beat the tar out of Jackson. The other kids watched and debated what may have caused such a fight, but none of them would say it was wrong.

The playground fell into chaos. The big rubber balls didn't go boing, boing, boing anymore, and there were no more baseball games. No one wanted to play by the rules, and most denied there were any rules at all, so no one played. There were no rules except Tracy's. There was no longer any fun either.

This story about an imaginary playground illustrates what happens when people abandon morality based on Someone outside themselves. When people get rid of God and morality, when they say that God is irrelevant and morality is old-fashioned, then it's like the playground without Mrs. Kravitz. The rules are abandoned. In their place are values created by people—often the most powerful and evil people on the playground.

If God exists and rules this universe, then we have in God a source for meaning, value, and dignity, and an objective way to separate right from wrong. But if we attempt to remove God from our thinking, then we have none of these things, and neither do our children.

Interestingly, John H. Hoover and Ronald Oliver, two authors for the National Educational Service, recognize the relationship between abusive behavior and the absence of spiritual values. In *The Bullying Prevention Handbook,* Hoover and Oliver point out:

> In the end, bullying is related to our ultimate beliefs about the worth of individuals and the way they should be treated. The topics of morality, moral education, ethical reasoning, and spirituality lie at the core of society's problems, including child-on-child aggression. As practitioners think about bullying in the future, it would be beneficial to examine the role that moral development plays in learning to care about one another. Educational leaders may look to the world's religions for answers to the problems of how we interrelate. For example, the Judeo-Christian-Islamic view that man is created in the image of God has enormous moral implications for how the weakest among us are treated. In the Christian tradition,

Jesus stated that whatever was done to the weakest was done to him.[2]

Yes! The antidote to our playground chaos can be found in religious faith and values. But interestingly, the very thing that these authors say is key to morality is banned in most schools. In removing religion from American schools, school administrators have also removed an important basis for telling kids that they must treat each other with respect.

The truth is, of course, that we all know what fairness and justice mean. Even little children know about fairness, and most of them have never taken a philosophy class or majored in theology.

"Johnny, put that cookie away; you'll spoil your supper."

"But Susie gets to have one!"

Even kids who have not been raised with religion still know when they're being ripped off. I suggest that every human being is born with a sense of justice because every human being, whether they acknowledge it or not, is made in the image of God. God is a moral God, a moral law Giver, and he has written his moral law on the heart of every human being.

When people try to get around this, it makes for a wacky world:

"It's wrong to impose your morals on others!"

Uh . . . pardon me, but when you tell me it's wrong to do something, aren't you imposing your morals on me?

"There are no absolutes."
That in itself is an absolute statement!

"You can't know anything for sure."
You seem rather sure about that.

"Students, no view of reality is superior to any other."
Then why are you *grading* our papers?

"There is no right; there is no wrong."
Is that statement right or wrong?

See what I mean? A lot of this stuff can get pretty silly, especially for those of us who ascribe to a biblical code of ethics. The simple truth is that we cannot build an argument against objective truth and morality without falling back on objective truth and morality!

Some folks will give a speech about open-mindedness and deny absolute truth or morality—until someone crowds in front of them in the grocery checkout line. They will scoff at such antiquated ideas as honor, virtue, and integrity—until a burglar ransacks their home. Then, suddenly, they will appeal to absolutes: "That's not fair! I've been cheated, robbed, violated!"

Oh, yeah? Who says?

I believe that God says. God, the external, objective Giver of truth and morality, says that some things are right and some things are wrong. As the prophet Micah tells it,

The LORD has told you, human,
     what is good;
he has told you what he wants from you:
to do what is right to other people,
love being kind to others,
and live humbly, obeying your God. (6:8)

I believe that every human being has value, meaning, and dignity. Why? Because we matter to Almighty God! Moreover, not only is it wrong for me to devalue another person, to belittle, to bully, or to abuse another person, but I must do what I can to defend those who cannot defend themselves from such abuse. We really are "family," whether or not we choose to admit it.

What people call "the Golden Rule" really comes from Jesus who said, "Do to others what you want them to do to you. This is the meaning of the law of Moses and the teaching of the prophets" (Matthew 7:12).

That's not a bad code to live by.

6
Have You Been Hurt?

When I told a friend of mine that I was writing a book about teasing and peer abuse, he quipped, "Oh, so you're writing a book about life!" He had a point there. Quite simply, garbage does happen, and we've all been touched by it in some form at one time or another. Most of us have been teased, have done the teasing, or both. So the question is, how do we get over the pain? How do we deal with the wounds inside? What can we do about the hurtful situations we're in right now? Here's what I've discovered.

First of all, if you're wounded, *you're not alone.* Obvious, right? But before you shrug this little truism off as just another trite phrase or cutesy emotional Band-Aid, please consider how normal it makes you.

People come in all shapes and sizes, with all kinds of different abilities and disabilities: Some are slim; some are fat; others are handsome, ugly, inferior, strong, weak, dorky, or nerdy, but God made us all. That makes every one of us special, despite our shortcomings. All of us have something, or lack something, that potentially can make us a target for abuse.

Everybody has something they wish they could change about themselves. If you have discovered some defect in yourself—welcome to the human race. Regardless of your failures, foibles, or defeats, you're just as human (and just as precious) as anybody else. You're a member of the human race.

Do you think you're ugly? You're a member.

Do you have cystic hygroma, cerebral palsy, hyperactivity, or asthma? You're a member.

Do you have freckles? Are you too tall, too skinny, too much . . . anything? You're a member.

Do you feel left out simply because you're smart? You're a member.

Have you ever been raped? Molested? You're a member.

You're a member of the human race.

And here's another startling revelation: *It wasn't (isn't) your fault.* One of the most common mistakes made by victims of abuse is to think that for some reason the abuse was justified. Nothing could be farther from the truth!

This came as a real lightning bolt for me while I was working on this book. As I reluctantly trudged back through my dark, difficult memories and encountered the faces and voices of my abusers, I finally saw them for what they were: bullies, not to be feared but to be pitied. Suddenly it dawned on me: It wasn't my fault! What those kids did to me had nothing to do with me. There was never anything so terribly wrong with me that other people had no choice but to be irresistibly, uncontrollably compelled to abuse me. I was not some freak of nature who merited the disdain with which I was treated. It wasn't my problem; it was theirs!

I guess it's just one of those quirky, human tendencies: We tend to believe what others say about us and to view ourselves through their eyes. The moment we get around other people, we start wondering, *Am I okay? Are they going to like me? Will they accept me?* If we manage to make a good impression and everybody seems to like us, we usually go home feeling pretty good about ourselves.

On the other hand, if we stumble or make a blunder, if somebody in the room brands us as the fool or the whole gang of them ignores us entirely, it's quite easy to go home believing we are what they have made us out to be.

When I was in junior high, I was very small for my age. That shouldn't have been a problem, but of course there were those in my class who made it a problem, as if there were something wrong with me for being small. Well, I believed it. After all, it was my smallness. I was the one who brought it to school with me. If I was being heckled, bullied, and thrown around, it was because I deserved it. If I'd just had the common sense to be bigger before coming to school, the other kids would have had no choice but to accept me. No one has the right to be small. I should have known that.

Weird, isn't it? For some reason we focus on ourselves as the cause of the abuse, as if our tormentors have no choice (or responsibility) in the matter, and we buy into their program of lies and humiliation. Before long, we begin thinking, I'm no good. I'm dumb. I'm a fool. I'm a shrimp. I'm a klutz. That's what the bullies say, so it has to be true!

You're not perfect, and that's okay! Nobody's perfect,

and if anybody ever made an issue of it, they were the ones in the wrong, not you. To put it simply, what happened to you shouldn't have happened. What was said about you shouldn't have been said, and what was done to you shouldn't have been done. Nobody deserves to be abused. So please don't blame yourself.

Now the third important observation is this: *You don't have to put up with it.* Looking back, one of the greatest mysteries of my life is why I put up with the abuse for so long. I can only explain it this way: I thought I had to. Most of what I endured happened at school. There was no way I could avoid school. While transferring to another district, attending private school, or home-schooling may be viable options for some families today, these were not options for my family. I was stuck in that school. My parents made me go. The teachers made me sit at my desk. I was a good kid trying to be obedient. No one ever told me, "Frank, you're in school to learn, not to be picked on and tormented. Teasing and abuse are not part of the package, and we won't allow it. We care about you, so if anyone causes you trouble, let us know."

No one said that to me so I had to speak up for myself. You can, too. Stand up. Speak up. You don't have to tolerate the abuse any longer. But you may have to take the first step, at least you must be ready to respond when you see an opportunity to bring the abuse to the attention of the proper authorities.

Because so much of the torment that I suffered from occurred in gym class, I never expected much compassion or mercy from my gym teachers. But all that changed when one man, a gym teacher, took the time to care. It started one day when I was running an errand for my mom to the corner grocery.

I was minding my own business, just going up and down the short aisles and picking up items on my grocery list, when a kid from school who worked there met me toward the back of the store, out of his boss's earshot. I was pleased when he seemed to be offering to help me and started to hand me the can of deodorant I'd been reaching for. But instead, without provocation, he popped the cap off and sprayed the deodorant directly in my face! I forget what he said as he did it, but it wasn't kind. And that stuff stings! My eyes started watering and flooding with tears. I was shocked and incredulous. I made a hasty exit from the store.

As I stumbled out of the store and around the corner, something broke inside me. I dropped to the curb, devastated, despondent. I'd come to the end. *Oh, dear God,* I prayed, still wiping the sting out of my eyes. *Please . . . I just can't take it anymore.* It felt a little strange to be praying such a thing because I still linked God with all the other authorities in my life. They were all making me go through this, including God. So, as I prayed, I was actually pleading for mercy. *Please, God, please don't do this to me anymore. Don't make me go back there. Have mercy. I haven't fought back; I haven't snitched; haven't I suffered enough?*

And, after so, so, long, God answered me. A few days later I faithfully and obediently stepped through the big, ominous door for another hour of gym. My despair must have been showing. One of the teachers paused—he actually took just a moment—and spoke quietly to me. "How you doing? You feeling okay?"

I looked back at him in disbelief. Somebody in authority was actually asking about me, and he seemed genuinely concerned! He wasn't even my teacher. He had other classes, other coaching duties, but he was there, and he had noticed that I was looking ill.

I didn't know what to say or whether to say anything at all. I was afraid of those gruff gym teachers. Not one of them had ever before asked me how I felt.

I muttered something, and he went on about his business. But the gentle tone of his voice did something to me: It gave me the tiniest ray of hope, something I'd never felt before. Somebody really wanted to know how I was doing! Somebody might really listen! I grabbed onto that hope for all I was worth, and then an idea came to me. I didn't think I could express myself orally to a teacher who still intimidated me, but by now I knew I could write. I decided to write my gym teacher a letter. I would tell him everything. Maybe things could change.

The first chance I got, I started drafting a letter to Mr. Sampson, my gym teacher. First I let him know that it was the kind inquiry of his colleague that prompted my letter, and then I began. I wrote during every opportunity I could find. I chronicled everything I could remember: all the insults, the abuse, the assaults, the humiliations, everything over the past several years. The letter filled several pages, handwritten in blue ink, single-spaced, both sides of the paper. Then I went to the school office and slipped it into Mr. Sampson's mailbox.

Gym class was every other day, so he had a day to read my letter before I had to face him again. By the time I came through that door the next time, Mr. Sampson was looking for me. "Peretti. Hold up a second," he called from inside his locker-room office.

Well, Mr. Sampson had obviously read my letter. Now what? He didn't seem very angry. Who else had seen that letter? What if he wanted to read the letter in front of the other guys in the locker room! *Oh, Lord, please don't let me down.*

Mr. Sampson filled out a hall pass and sent me to the school office to see the counselor, Mr. Eisenbrey. I'd always been afraid of Mr. Sampson, and I'd always been afraid of Mr. Eisenbrey, but that day changed everything. Those guys had compassion on me. They really did care. Mr. Eisenbrey had reviewed my letter and was actually warm and cheerful as he helped me rework my class schedule, excusing me from gym for the remainder of the school year. "We'll just call it a medical excuse," he said, scribbling some notes on a piece of paper. He signed me off and sent me back to Mr. Sampson so he could sign the forms, too. Mr. Sampson didn't say anything as he filled out the form on his clipboard. He just smiled at me.

When he handed me my class transfer, my parole, I told him, "If you were a girl, I'd kiss you!"

"You're welcome," was all he said, smiling. I went out that door and never saw the inside of that locker room again.

I can't overstate the pivotal nature of that day in my life. From that moment onward, everything was different. I could enjoy school. I could get excited about being a Cleveland Eagle. I bought a red-and-white pennant and put it on my bedroom wall. I donned my red-and-white Cleveland beanie, went to the football games, and felt great about my school. I got involved in school drama productions—where I could actually use some of the gifts God had given me. I burst out of my shell, making lots of new friends and going nuts being creative. For the first time in my life, I began to enjoy being me!

The point is this: Someone in your school, neighborhood, or wherever will be kind to you. They will have the caring, compassionate attitude that is necessary to bring about a change. Talk about what is happening. I understand that the expectation of our culture has been to keep it to yourself. If you think you need some kind of permission to bring up the subject and deal with it, I give you that permission now. Get help! Talk to someone who might care. Don't go another day carrying the burden alone. If the first person you talk to does not help, then try someone else. If you have to call the police and report it, then do it, but keep talking!

In addition to talking to someone in authority, try talking to the bully. Granted, some bullies cannot be talked to at all. They pick on you because they are warped and maladjusted. For any number of reasons—a dysfunctional family, low self-esteem, low achievement, too much lead in their drinking water, or some other malady—they think they have to push their weight around in order to feel better about themselves. Unless they have a major turnaround in their lives, they'll either wind up in prison or become driver's license examiners.

But for the most part, bullies are human beings just like you and me, and sometimes they can be reached with a little bit of honesty and friendship, *if* you can talk with them one-on-one. I've known a few bullies who were actually very intelligent *A* students, who went on to be successful adults. Oftentimes, the reason they allowed themselves to become cruel and insensitive was because of the crowd; it was the "cool" thing to do.

Consider going to that person and having a private discussion with him, away from his friends. Be sincere, kind, and honest, and lay the issues on the table: You would rather be friends than enemies, and what he is doing is hurtful to you. If you have done something to offend him, apologize and make it right. If you've done nothing to offend him, ask him why he wants to hurt you.

Attempt to get to know the person who has been bullying you. In nine cases out of ten, bullies don't even know the person they're picking on. If they really knew the victim as a person instead of as a punching bag, they might ease up. Who knows? You could end up being friends.

If you can't approach the bully directly, perhaps you and the bully have a mutual friend or acquaintance to whom you could appeal for help. I remember sitting at lunch with a friend named Paul in junior high school, and I started sharing my problems with him.

"Who's picking on you?" he asked.

I didn't have any trouble thinking of a name. I could even point the guy out, sitting across the lunchroom. "He's really mean. He just won't leave me alone."

Paul was astonished. "Neil? Are you sure?"

I told Paul what Neil had been doing to me in the locker room during gym class, and Paul shook his head, perplexed. He was genuinely surprised and dismayed to hear about the way Neil had been treating me. "But Neil's a nice guy."

"Well, he sure isn't nice to me," I replied.

The next time I encountered Neil in the locker room, he was friendly. He complimented the sweater I was wearing. He never badgered, bullied, or bothered me again!

It's easy to figure out what happened. Paul went to Neil and told him, "Hey, Frank's a decent guy. He's a friend of mine. Don't pick on him."

Dealing with a wounded spirit means dealing with the abuse and refusing to allow it to continue. Guess what else it means? *Forgiving the bully!* What?! Why should I forgive the bully? The answer is simple: If you don't forgive those individuals who have hurt you in the past, you will be granting the bullies the power to take away your happiness in the future! Unforgiveness leads to bitterness and that can destroy your happiness. Throw off those chains of bitterness and resentment and get on with your life.

Finally, take heart: *A wounded spirit need not be permanent.* Life as we know it right now is not fixed in cement. As we grow, we change, our circumstances change, and we find ourselves in different places and situations. When I was a kid, I felt terrible about myself. My self-image was in the toilet because I couldn't throw or catch a football, I couldn't run very fast, and I was considered small and frail for my age. Today, I'm an adult. I'm an author and a public speaker, I play in a band, I fly my own plane, I have a lovely wife, and I own a comfortable home tucked in the woods on the side of a mountain. And you know what? I still can't throw or catch a football!

Every once in a while, as I sit in our living room, looking out the picture windows and admiring the beauty of the snowcapped mountains, I wonder how many of those big jocks I once knew are now limping from old sports injuries. I can't help but smile as I picture some of them reporting to short bosses with much bigger offices! As Bill Gates has said, "Don't pick on the nerds. You'll probably end up working for one."

7
For the Bullies

Until now, I've been writing from the perspective of the victim, which puts me in a safe place. I can be the sweet, innocent hero of the story, while all the other characters are the bad guys. Well, it was nice while it lasted, but in real life there is always another side to the story. Whether we regard ourselves as bully or victim, we're all made of the same stuff. We're all capable of the same things.

Have I ever wounded anyone? I'm sorry to say that I have. I never considered myself the bullying type, but there were times when I could say mean things. I could spread malicious gossip, cut people down with insults, or go along with the crowd in ostracizing someone. It's so easy to do, and it amazes me how a victim, who knows how it feels, can still be insensitive to the feelings of others. Know what I'm talking about?

So . . . this could get uncomfortable, but let's be honest as we work through this chapter together. Most of us have been wounded by other people, some of us have wounded others, and some of us have not only been wounded, but for whatever reason go on to wound others!

Wounding other people comes naturally. We don't feel

the pain as we dish it out, so we go along with the attitude that says, "It's no big deal. All my friends are picking on so-and-so, and I want to be accepted as one of
the group." We know better, yet we don't act the way we
know we should.

Even goody-goody church people wound. Let's talk
about all those squeaky-clean students attending conser-
vative colleges. They know their Bibles. They worship
and pray at all the chapel services. They're out to spread
the good news and change their world for the glory of
God. And yet, when you get a chance to observe the
social fabric on campus, it's sad to discover that things
haven't changed much since junior and senior high
school. The upperclassmen find it easy to put the un-
derclassmen in their place. The jocks laugh and needle
the nonathletes; the girls establish their social cliques and
close the door to outsiders. Derogatory names and ru-
mors float around freely. The very mention of certain
names produces snickers among the elite in the student
lounge.

On any college campus, it's normal to find a particular type of young male who takes pride in his physical
prowess but seems stunted when it comes to character.
He shoots baskets but doesn't help the kid who would
like to learn; he presses iron but never thinks of coaching anyone else; he flexes his muscles and disrespects
anyone who doesn't.

I encountered a young man of this description some
time ago, and he was the quintessential bullying jock.
I'd never before seen someone purposely wearing a tight
muscle shirt and flexing his muscles at everybody. I
thought only professional wrestlers did that! This guy

could even make his neck bigger than his head, and he was really proud of that.

Unfortunately, along with all those muscles came a bad attitude. This fellow had the idea that his finely chiseled, powerful physique entitled him to be the king in any group. I saw him grab a smaller guy, lift him off his feet, and pin him against the wall, purely to intimidate him. Mind you, this incident took place among young men at an elite religious college! I must have been naive at the time because it shocked me so severely that I didn't say a word.

I am reminded of the film *A Few Good Men.* The movie unfortunately has some coarse language and so I can't recommend it for kids, but that movie has powerful moral lessons. The story involves two marines, stationed at a military base, who are ordered by their superior officer to carry out a "code red" on a fellow marine. A "code red" is an unofficial, even illegal form of discipline that can take the form of a beating, hazing, or any other humiliation, and the purpose is to "encourage" a soldier to get his act together. The soldier in this case was a weakling named Willie who had a medical condition that prevented him from keeping up with the other soldiers when they were running in the stifling heat on the base. But neither Willie nor anyone else knew he had this medical condition—until it was too late. As Willie is "encouraged" to shape up, his medical condition kills him, and the two marines are put on trial for murder.

Thus arise some great moral issues and some great quotes. The defendants' lawyers work together as a team even though they are divided regarding the marines' innocence. One thinks the two marines are innocent because they were following orders, but another feels that is no excuse: "I believe every word of their story—and I think they ought to go to jail for the rest of their lives. . . . They beat up on a weakling! That's all they did, all right? . . . They tortured and tormented a weaker kid! They didn't like him, so they killed him, and why? 'Cause he couldn't run very fast!"

As the trial ends, the marines are acquitted of murder, but they are convicted of conduct unbecoming a marine and are sentenced to be dishonorably discharged from the Marine Corps. The younger marine protests, "I don't understand. Colonel Jessup said he ordered the code red. What did we do wrong? We did nothing wrong!"

But the older marine responds, "Yeah, we did. We were supposed to fight for people who couldn't fight for themselves. We were supposed to fight for Willie." By this point in the movie, I get tearful. This is the answer. This is what it's all about. The filmmakers have addressed something that we who spend most of our lives in safe confines rarely confront. Namely, the depth of a person's character is not measured by his or her physical strength, but by the depth of his or her nobility: How do you treat those who are weaker?

After thinking about the issue of protecting the weak, I have replayed in my mind what I should have done on that college campus when I saw the muscleman abuse another student: I should have stepped up to that big lug, looked him right in the eyes and said, "Just what in the world do you think you're doing? You stop that immediately!"

And then I'd grab a telephone—in my mental replay, a phone is always handy—and tell that muscleman, "See this phone in my hand? You have a choice. Either you sit down and listen to a lecture, or I dial the police and file a criminal complaint against you for assault. Which will it be?"

He agrees to the lecture. Having his undivided attention, I tell him, "God gave you all that strength and physical superiority. It wasn't so you could abuse, oppress, and violate those who aren't as strong. Any gift you receive from God is not for yourself, but for others. The strong are to protect the weak; those with abundance are blessed so they can help the needy; the smart and wise are gifted to help the befuddled and foolish."

All it takes is a decision, a pivotal moment when you decide you will put a stop to the bullying and abuse and begin treating everyone who passes your way as a priceless creation of God.

The first step to stop bullying is to *wake up to what you've done* and what you may still be doing. I can still see the faces of some of the people I hurt. How about you? How many faces can you count? Are you inflicting wounds on others? How do you want people to remember you?

Second, you need to *get rid of your guilt*. For me that means going to God in prayer and asking him to bring to my mind the folks I've hurt. Then I've apologized to God in prayer, asking God to grant each person the grace to forgive me and to help them find healing in their lives. When it was possible, I have found that person I hurt and apologized in person. I also asked God to change my heart and make me open and loving.

Finally, you might consider how you can *show more gratitude* for whatever advantage you have: your physical strength, your intelligence, your sense of humor, your reputation, that position on the cheerleading squad or the football team, or the opened doors of opportunity at your job.

You can put your gift into service on behalf of others. You can become, in your own way, the guardian who stands on the wall and says to those who are weaker, smaller, and less advantaged, "Don't you worry. Nobody's going to hurt you, not on my watch."

8
The Way It Should Be

A separate room had been prepared for the boys. It was cold and impersonal; the echoing, concrete walls had been painted beige, then marred and chipped over the years, and then painted again. The walls were bare except for posted rules, warnings, and advisories, and the only windows were high against the ceiling, caged behind iron grillwork thickly wrapped in paint, rust, and more paint. The air was dank, tainted with the odors of steam, sweat, and skin. Years of rust and sediment from the dripping showerheads and armies of bare, wet feet had marbled the floor with streaks and patches of reddish brown.

The boy was nervous and afraid on his first day through that big door. He was small and timid. Though he excelled in academics and felt comfortable in most classrooms, to him this was a different, threatening world, a world of muscles and sweat. As he lined up along the lockers with the other boys his age, he could see some of them sizing him up. "Hi, wimp," one of them said, a sneer curling his lip.

"Hey!" It was the teacher's assistant, a few grades older, overseeing the lineup. He went over to the kid who'd spoken and got right in his face. "You don't do that in here."

The name-caller was about to come back with something, but a shrill whistle made him jump.

It was the gym teacher, Mr. Akers, entering the locker room like an officer coming on deck. "All right, silence! Everybody, eyes forward and pay attention!"

He got immediate compliance, and with good enough reason. This guy was built like a tank, and his expression made it clear he was not to be trifled with. He carried a clipboard. He had a whistle around his neck. He wore a tight T-shirt.

"Mr. Lane will take the roll."

The teacher's assistant, Bruce Lane, called out the names of the students and checked them off as they answered, "Here." All through the roll call, Mr. Akers stood there with his clipboard and his whistle, studying every face.

When the roll call ended, he said, "At ease. Have a seat on the benches, fellows. Make room over there. Let's go."

They sat down facing him. He leaned against the wall, one foot flat on the wall behind him so that his knee extended, forming a desk for his clipboard. "Gentlemen, welcome to my class. On your class schedule you see this hour designated as 'Physical Education,' but let me assure you, this class will involve more than just your bodies. Any education worthy of the name doesn't just build the body or the mind; it also builds character. So you'll need more than a strong body and athletic skill to excel in this class—sorry to disappoint some of you. You'll need to apply your minds and your spirits as well.

"It is our hope that you'll leave here healthier and more physically fit than when you first came in. But it is also our hope that you'll leave here having improved the personal qualities you'll need in every other area of your lives: discipline, perseverance, the ability and willingness to work as a team, and a sportsmanlike attitude.

"If you enjoy competition, I encourage you to turn out for the basketball, baseball, football, tennis, or soccer teams. I assure you, in those programs you will have every opportunity to one-up the guy on the opposing team and show everybody what a great athlete you are. In this class, the only person you'll be competing against is yourself. We're going to help you set reasonable goals for improving your fitness, strength, and stamina, and then we're going to do all we can to help you achieve those goals.

"Now as you look around the room, you'll notice that human beings come in all sizes and shapes, all different levels of strength and ability. I want to emphasize that none of that matters here. Regardless of your size or physical maturity, each and every one of you deserves the chance to feel proud of what you can accomplish. That's why we're going to be a team. We're going to think as a team, act as a team, and learn as a team. We expect you to help each other out, to cheer for each other, to do all you can to help your teammates rise to their potential.

"That's why we do not tolerate bullies in this class. We do not allow teasing, harassment, put-downs, one-upmanship, or the mistreatment of any teammate by another." He paused to let that sink in, and then added,

"You will maintain sportsmanlike conduct at all times, showing courtesy and respect for your teammates."

The boy had come into this class feeling timid and afraid, but by the time Mr. Akers had finished his orientation remarks, he could see he had an advocate if he ever needed one. He was starting to feel safe.

In the weeks that followed, Mr. Akers and his assistants worked with each class member, planning out a fitness program appropriate to each boy's ability. Because of his small stature and clumsiness, the boy had always been intimidated by any sport that threw him among bodies bigger than his. The workout room with its treadmill, stepper, and weight machine appealed to him because he could work on his own without embarrassment.

"Just remember," Mr. Akers told him, "you're not here to be like somebody else. You're here to improve yourself and to help the others do the same." With encouragement from Mr. Akers, the young man set reasonable goals for himself. With encouragement from his classmates, he exceeded those goals. On the last day of the semester, he cheered for his classmates, and they cheered for him.

He didn't think he'd ever look forward to gym class, but by semester's end, he decided he could enjoy it. What a class!

Imagine a school that openly, directly enforced an anti-bullying policy, instructing and encouraging kids to call witnesses and to back each other up when a bullying incident occured. Imagine students being instructed that they are responsible for their fellow human beings and that it is right and noble to get involved when someone is being hurt. Imagine a student being able to attend school knowing that his or her classmates, whether friend or stranger, are there to help.

Is this imaginary school impossible? No. We just have to work on it.

❖❖❖❖❖

As I've worked on this book, I've found it comforting to think that after thirty or forty years, I can finally make some good use of all that trouble I went through. God does not waste an ounce of our pain or a drop of our tears; suffering doesn't come our way for no reason, and God seems especially efficient at using what we endure to mold our character. Our bumps and bruises become something beautiful.

Having experienced how sour this world can be, I've tried to spread around as much sugar as I can. If I encounter a waitress having a bad day, I try to be as nice to her as I can be, and I usually leave a generous tip. It's a tangible way of saying, "You're doing a good job, and I appreciate you." Have you ever worked at a fast-food restaurant? If so, you probably have a greater appreciation for that young man or woman behind the counter who is trying to juggle several orders while customers wait impatiently. No doubt some irate customer has already yelled at my waitress for spilling something or counting the change wrong. I'd like to be the nice customer she has that day, the customer who gives her a break.

I try to use humor and display goodwill toward everyone with whom I do business, from bank clerks to telephone operators to delivery truck drivers. People appreciate kindness. Pass some sugar around, and others will throw some sugar back to you.

Comforting others puts our pain into perspective. Having encountered others who have suffered rapes, domestic violence, permanent disfigurement from disease or birth defect, molestation, and violent crime, I can tell myself, "Okay. You had some tough times, but be thankful. Compared to many people in this world, you had it easy."

I'm convinced that cruelty in and of itself is not fruitful, and to the fullest extent of my power, I won't allow it. I'm not impressed by the old argument that cruelty toughens us up for life. That's tantamount to saying it's right. Life is cruel enough by itself, thank you, with endless opportunities to suffer. Given that, one kind word or one encouraging touch teaches more lessons than one hundred cruelties.

Maybe we're entering a new era in which bullying and the intimidation of other people are at last consigned to their rightful place alongside racism, hate-mongering, drunk driving, littering, spitting in public, and passing gas at parties.

People are slowly waking up to the prolonged impact of the problem—that bullies in school often grow up to be bullies in the home, abusing their spouses and children and perpetuating the downward spiral. Bullies in the home leave the house and go to work, where they continue to abuse employees and coworkers. The cycle can only be stopped by a change of the heart, and that is precisely the place where God's power is more than sufficient to give people a fresh start. With other options exhausted, some people are beginning to give the spiritual solution serious thought. Let's encourage more of that, and while we're at it, let's search our own hearts and instruct others about what it means to be noble, to protect and help the weak, to love our neighbors—even the smaller and clumsier ones—as ourselves.

notes

[1]Suellen Fried and Paula Fried, *Bullies and Victims* (New York: Evans and Co., 1996), 87.

[2]John H. Hoover and Ronald Oliver, *The Bullying Prevention Handbook: A Guide for Principals, Teachers, and Counselors* (Bloomington, IN: National Educational Service, 1996), 96–97.